BOSS
LADY
BELIEVER

DEVOTIONAL FOR
BUSINESS WOMEN

BY ANGELA
Walsh

JEREMIAH 29:11
[11] For I know the plans I have for you, says the LORD. They are plans for good and not for disaster, to give you a future and a hope.

Work Like a Boss... Act Like a Lady...Live Like a Believer

ABOUT THE AUTHOR

Angela Walsh lives in Texas with her husband, mother, and two teenage daughters. The house is also full of a variety of furry children that bring joy to their lives.

After graduating from Stephen F. Austin State University, she began her professional career as an early childhood specialist, with a focus on early education and reading.

After a few years of battling serious health conditions, she retired from the education world and focused on her first passion- writing and reaching out to other Christian businesswomen.

The main purpose of Boss Lady Believer was to help professional businesswomen find strength and encouragement when facing obstacles in a mainstream world.

Her next focus will be on bringing help and awareness to at-risk children, with a huge emphasis on providing homes, families, and resources to women and girls affected by abuse, neglect, addiction, and the horrendous acts of sex trafficking.

If you would like to be involved with helping children, please visit: ImagineFoundationForKids.Org

25% of sales from this book go to establishing a fund to help provide homes and resources for the Imagine Foundation For Kids.

Make sure to visit the book website at:

www.bossladybeliever.com

Work Like a Boss... Act Like a Lady...Live Like a Believer

Work Like a Boss... Act Like a Lady...Live Like a Believer

CONTENTS

Work Like a Boss... Act Like a Lady...Live Like a Believer

ACKNOWLEDGMENTS

All glory to my Father God, who always believed and encouraged me, even during moments when I turned away from Him.

Thank you to my family for allowing me time to focus on writing, encouraging me, and giving me the confidence to know that this project would be completed.

Finally, thank you to all of the businesswomen and men who aren't afraid to express their Christian beliefs in a world where materialism and stepping on others to succeed is so common.

Bible verses are taken from the New Living Translation version of the Holy Bible

You can run your business and still have faith as your foundation.

You can be open about your faith and be confident in your beliefs.

It's okay to be a Christian businesswoman and not hide your faith from your customers and network.

God will guide you.

Work Like a Boss... Act Like a Lady...Live Like a Believer

CHAPTER ONE

BELIEVING IN THE GIFTS GOD HAS GIVEN YOU

JEREMIAH 29:11
[11] For I know the plans I have for you, says the LORD.
They are plans for good and not for disaster,
to give you a future and a hope.

You have a gift that was bestowed upon you even before you were
placed on this earth. The problem arises when we are taught to
ignore those inherent feelings and listen to what society tells us is the
appropriate path for our lives.
God has a reason for you to be here.
No one is greater, more special, or more deserving.
We all have a plan.

We all matter in the eyes of Father God.

Close your eyes and imagine yourself being happy.
What comes to mind when you think about this?
Write a note below on what you are feeling right now.

Notes---

My Prayers:

Answers to Prayer:

MATTHEW 6:21
[21] **Wherever your treasure is,**
there the desires of your heart will also be.

What is your "go to" activity?
Do you always lean towards writing, singing, helping others,
creating things, managing and supervising, beauty, teaching others, or
something else?
There are so many things that can be added to this list.

In the space below, record the things that you *think* about doing,
or the things you *wish* you had more time to do.

Notes---

My Prayers:

Answers to Prayer:

1 CORINTHIANS 12:4-7

[4] **There are different kinds of spiritual gifts, but the same Spirit is the source of them all. [5] There are different kinds of service, but we serve the same Lord. [6] God works in different ways, but it is the same God who does the work in all of us. [7] A spiritual gift is given to each of us so we can help each other.**

Do you realize that you were made for, and with, a purpose?
Think about that one... YOU have a PURPOSE.

One God... Many People... Many Gifts

Imagine using those gifts as the foundation for your business. Do you think you would struggle as much if you were living each day using the gifts given? If you were fulfilling your true purpose, defining your life the way it was meant to be, and not being ashamed of anything done in HIS name, you would be so fulfilled and ready to encourage others.

Make a list of what you truly enjoy, then think of how you can create a life around that list. Do what you love, and you'll never "work" a day of your life again.

Notes---

My Prayers:

Answers to Prayer:

PROVERBS 16:3
**³ Commit your actions to the LORD,
and your plans will succeed.**

How are you using your gifts to help others?
How do you know what your gifts are?

Think about it... are there things that come naturally to you? Things
that you enjoy? Things that motivate you and drive you to do better?

You were not made to drudge through a miserable existence.
You have God-given gifts that were created to make life better and
glorify the One who created us.

Notes---

My Prayers:

Answers to Prayer:

CHAPTER TWO

FAITH AND PERSEVERANCE

2 TIMOTHY 4:2-5

[2] **Preach the word of God. Be prepared, whether the time is favorable or not. Patiently correct, rebuke, and encourage your people with good teaching.**

[3] **For a time is coming when people will no longer listen to sound and wholesome teaching. They will follow their own desires and will look for teachers who will tell them whatever their itching ears want to hear.**

[4] **They will reject the truth and chase after myths.**

[5] **But you should keep a clear mind in every situation. Don't be afraid of suffering for the Lord. Work at telling others the Good News, and fully carry out the ministry God has given you.**

Have you noticed how many interpretations there are for the exact same verse in the Bible? Anything can be molded and twisted to fit a person's wants and desires, to justify any form of thinking, or to validate what they know is morally wrong.

Don't get caught up in the worship of man or self.

Notes---

My Prayers:

Answers to Prayer:

1 CORINTHIANS 9:24

[24] Don't you realize that in a race everyone runs, but only one person gets the prize? So run to win!

How does an athlete prepare for a race?
What sacrifices do you need to make in order to prepare yourself for the blessings ahead? Are there things in your life that you need to work on so that you'll be ready when that day comes?

Notes---

My Prayers:

Answers to Prayer:

ROMANS 5:3-4

[3] **We can rejoice, too, when we run into problems and trials, for we know that they help us develop endurance.**
[4] **And endurance develops strength of character, and character strengthens our confident hope of salvation.**

In the space below, reflect on moments of suffering that resulted in making you stronger and caused you to rely heavily on God to pull you through.

Notes---

My Prayers:

Answers to Prayer:

MARK 5:36
**³⁶ But Jesus overheard them and said to Jairus,
Don't be afraid. Just have faith.**

Pray ~ Trust ~ Believe
Sounds easy, doesn't it?

What obstacles do you face when you try to give it all over to God?
God is big enough to create the world.
He's definitely big enough to handle your life.
Believe

Notes---

Work Like a Boss... Act Like a Lady...Live Like a Believer

My Prayers:

Answers to Prayer:

CHAPTER THREE

RELYING ON GOD FOR SUCCESS

ROMANS 2:29

[29] ... And a person with a changed heart seeks praise from God, not from people.

If you lose business because of your beliefs, do not fret, because in time people will see that you are a person who does not compromise what you believe in, and that is far more valuable then one who flip flops with every person who walks through the door.

Stand firm – you are not in this alone.

Notes---

Work Like a Boss... Act Like a Lady...Live Like a Believer

My Prayers:

Answers to Prayer:

DEUTERONOMY 8:17-18

[17] **He did all this so you would never say to yourself, 'I have achieved this wealth with my own strength and energy.**

**'[18] Remember the LORD your God.
He is the one who gives you power to be successful,
in order to fulfill the covenant he confirmed
to your ancestors with an oath.**

It's easy to be caught up in the hustle and bustle of life once success finds you. Stay humble and find every opportunity to let others know that you are successful because of hard work and FAITH.

Notes---

My Prayers:

Answers to Prayer:

PROVERBS 3:34
**[34] The LORD mocks the mockers
but is gracious to the humble.**

Those that are quiet, or unobtrusive, are often mocked and criticized for not joining the crowd. Don't be afraid to keep to yourself, or to be quiet when under attack. The Lord sees and hears what is being done to you, trust Him to be in control.

Notes---

My Prayers:

Answers to Prayer:

PROVERBS 16:3
**[3] Commit your actions to the LORD,
and your plans will succeed.**

Sometimes, it's not all about what YOU want.
Be still, listen to that quiet voice that guides you, and pray for
guidance for every action.

Notes---

My Prayers:

Answers to Prayer:

CHAPTER FOUR

LOSING IT ALL TO GAIN IT ALL

ISAIAH 66:9
**[9] Would I ever bring this nation to the point of birth
and then not deliver it?, asks the LORD.
No! I would never keep this nation from being born,
says your God.**

God is not going to give you a gift and then
not allow you to use it for his kingdom.
Trust that the one who made you also made plans for you.

Notes---

My Prayers:

Answers to Prayer:

MARK 8:34-37

[34] **Then, calling the crowd to join his disciples, he said, If any of you wants to be my follower, you must give up your own way, take up your cross, and follow me.**
[35] **If you try to hang on to your life, you will lose it. But if you give up your life for my sake and for the sake of the Good News, you will save it.**
[36] **And what do you benefit if you gain the whole world but lose your own soul?**
[37] **Is anything worth more than your soul?**

It's hard to move on with the plans God has for you if you are still hanging on to the corner of a former life.
Think about it...
What do you need to let go of in order to fulfill your purpose?

Notes---

My Prayers:

Answers to Prayer:

ROMANS 12:12
**[12] Rejoice in our confident hope.
Be patient in trouble, and keep on praying.**

Have you lost everything you've owned, people you thought were
friends, and wondered how we were going to ever recover?
Your prayers and patience mold you into what God wants you to be.
A diamond is not beautiful at first, it takes a trained eye to chip away
and reveal the beauty.
What are you dealing with right now that requires
patience and prayer?

Notes---

Work Like a Boss... Act Like a Lady...Live Like a Believer

My Prayers:

Answers to Prayer:

PSALM 39:7
[7] And so, Lord, where do I put my hope?
My only hope is in you.

Days of hopelessness, feeling lost, unsure of where you are supposed
to be in your life, are sure to come. But, as believers, we have the
promise that our Father is going to take care of us.
Breathe...

Notes---

My Prayers:

Answers to Prayer:

CHAPTER FIVE

LONELINESS AND LET DOWNS

MATTHEW 10:22

[22] And all nations will hate you because you are my followers. But everyone who endures to the end will be saved.

What are some things you've had to endure because of your faith?

Notes---

My Prayers:

Answers to Prayer:

PROVERBS 15:13-14
**[13] A glad heart makes a happy face;
a broken heart crushes the spirit.
[14] A wise person is hungry for knowledge,
while the fool feeds on trash.**

Think about some trivial things that are out of your control.
Are you helping yourself by dwelling on them?
List some things you can take control of TODAY in
order to make each day more productive and positive.

Notes---

My Prayers:

Answers to Prayer:

LUKE 1:37
[37] For the word of God will never fail.

Do you trust that God is big enough to handle your problems?
Make a list of issues you are having difficulty with right now.
Pray over them, hand them over to God, and let go!

Notes---

My Prayers:

Answers to Prayer:

PSALM 27:10
**[10] Even if my father and mother abandon me,
the LORD will hold me close.**

It hurts when family members, even your own parents,
mock you for your beliefs.
When your entire support system lets you down, remember that your
Father God is always there for you.
He's just waiting for you to have a conversation with Him.

Notes---

My Prayers:

Answers to Prayer:

CHAPTER SIX

WORRYING ABOUT THE HURDLES

LUKE 12:22-26

[22] Then, turning to his disciples, Jesus said, That is why I tell you not to worry about everyday life—whether you have enough food to eat or enough clothes to wear. [23] For life is more than food, and your body more than clothing.
[24] Look at the ravens.
They don't plant or harvest or store food in barns, for God feeds them. And you are far more valuable to him than any birds! [25] Can all your worries add a single moment to your life? [26] And if worry can't accomplish a little thing like that, what's the use of worrying over bigger things?

What are your hurdles?

Notes---

Work Like a Boss... Act Like a Lady...Live Like a Believer

My Prayers:

Answers to Prayer:

MATTHEW 6:34

**[34] So don't worry about tomorrow,
for tomorrow will bring its own worries.**

Today's trouble is enough for today.

Circumstances can change in a heartbeat.
Take each day as it comes
and don't add to your burdens by worrying
about what hasn't happened.

Notes---

My Prayers:

Answers to Prayer:

JAMES 1:2-4

[2] Dear brothers and sisters, when troubles of any kind come
your way, consider it an opportunity for great joy.

[3] For you know that when your faith is tested,
your endurance has a chance to grow.
[4] So let it grow,
for when your endurance is fully developed,
you will be perfect and complete, needing nothing.

When do you find yourself praying the most?
Is it during those times when things are going smoothly,
or when you are in despair?

Notes---

My Prayers:

Answers to Prayer:

PSALM 142:1-2
¹I cry out to the LORD;
I plead for the LORD's mercy.
²I pour out my complaints before him
and tell him all my troubles.

What are some things you are facing each day?
Do you feel frustrated, angry, or hopeless?
Write down your worries, pray over them,
ask God to take them from you
and help you release control.
In a few months, go back over your list and
write down how each one was resolved.

Notes---

My Prayers:

Answers to Prayer:

CHAPTER SEVEN

BLESSINGS AND GIVING BACK

LUKE 6:38

[38] Give, and you will receive. Your gift will return to you in full— pressed down, shaken together to make room for more, running over, and poured into your lap. The amount you give will determine the amount you get back.

You may not have money in your pocket, but you have a smile that will help someone. You may not have material possessions to spare, but you can share a meal with someone.
Every blessing, even the small ones that you feel are insignificant, can mean the world to someone else.

Notes---

My Prayers:

Answers to Prayer:

1 PETER 4:10

[10] God has given each of you a gift from his great variety of spiritual gifts. Use them well to serve one another.

We are not meant to live, work, and die.
We are all given a gift, it can be gardening, drawing, singing,
or immense compassion for others.
What do you feel is your gift?
How could it be used to help others?

Notes---

My Prayers:

Answers to Prayer:

MATTHEW 5:16

¹⁶ In the same way, let your good deeds shine out for all to see, so that everyone will praise your heavenly Father.

We don't do good things for the praises of man.
We don't even do them to make ourselves shine.
A true good deed should reflect your daily actions, so that
when others do see you helping someone, they will know that
It is because you have
the heart of God and will praise Him.

Notes---

Work Like a Boss... Act Like a Lady...Live Like a Believer

My Prayers:

Answers to Prayer:

1 JOHN 3:17

[17] If someone has enough money to live well and sees a brother or sister in need but shows no compassion—how can God's love be in that person?

Who are you able to help today?
What are some things you can do for someone else
that doesn't require money?

Notes---

My Prayers:

Answers to Prayer:

Boss Lady Believer by Angela Walsh

CHAPTER EIGHT

GRATITUDE AND REMAINING HUMBLE

MARK 10:45

[45] For even the Son of Man came not to be served but to serve others and to give his life as a ransom for many.

Take today to look at life through Jesus' eyes.
What do you notice?

Notes---

Work Like a Boss... Act Like a Lady...Live Like a Believer

My Prayers:

Answers to Prayer:

PROVERBS 11:2
**[2] Pride leads to disgrace,
but with humility comes wisdom.**

Do you remember a moment when you thought you
knew all the answers? How did others treat you?

Notes---

My Prayers:

Answers to Prayer:

1 THESSALONIANS 5:18
[18] Be thankful in all circumstances, for this is God's will for you who belong to Christ Jesus.

We all have days where we beat ourselves up, wallow in pity, compare our lives to someone else who has more material items.
Step back, look at all you've been blessed with.
Think of others who would give anything to live your life.
Be thankful.

Notes---

My Prayers:

Answers to Prayer:

PSALMS 9:1
**¹I will praise you, LORD, with all my heart;
I will tell of all the marvelous things you have done.**

What's the point of having abundant blessings
if we don't share our testimony and gratefulness with others?
What marvelous things has God done for you?

Notes---

My Prayers:

Answers to Prayer:

CHAPTER NINE

BEING A GODLY BOSS

HEBREWS 13:7
[7] Remember your leaders who taught you the word of God. Think of all the good that has come from their lives, and follow the example of their faith.

Being a leader is a huge responsibility.
Every word and action is scrutinized and examined by someone at all times. Remain kind, humble, and fair. Remember to always give credit to God, who has blessed you abundantly and given you the responsibility of being a leader and an example to others.

Notes---

My Prayers:

Answers to Prayer:

MATTHEW 20:28

[28] For even the Son of Man came not to be served but to serve others and to give his life as a ransom for many.

A true leader is a servant to many.
How do you serve those around you?

Notes---

My Prayers:

Answers to Prayer:

1 PETER 5:2
**²Care for the flock that God has entrusted to you.
Watch over it willingly, not grudgingly—not for what you will
get out of it, but because you are eager to serve God.**

The responsibility of guiding and leading
is not one to be taken lightly.
Approach each task with the mindset of
keeping God first and foremost.
A Godly leader is one that cares for others with
humility, honesty, and love.
Never take that position for granted.

Notes---

Work Like a Boss... Act Like a Lady...Live Like a Believer

My Prayers:

Answers to Prayer:

MARK 10:43-44

[43] But among you it will be different. Whoever wants to be a leader among you must be your servant, [44] and whoever wants to be first among you must be the slave of everyone else.

Have you ever worked for someone that belittled you, made you feel less than others, and caused you to doubt your own abilities?
Don't be that kind of leader.
Reach out to those around you, show appreciation, and never think that you are too good to help them.

Notes---

My Prayers:

Answers to Prayer:

CHAPTER TEN

RESTING AND REJUVENATING

EXODUS 20:8-10

[8] **Remember to observe the Sabbath day by keeping it holy.** [9] **You have six days each week for your ordinary work,** [10] **but the seventh day is a Sabbath day of rest dedicated to the LORD your God.**
On that day no one in your household may do any work. This includes you, your sons and daughters, your male and female servants, your livestock, and any foreigners living among you.

Do you take time to reconnect with your
family, your own needs, and to refresh your body?
We are no good to anyone if exhaustion has taken over.
What are some things you can do each day to keep
your mind, body, and relationships from running on empty?

Notes---

My Prayers:

Answers to Prayer:

ECCLESIASTES 2:24-25
[24] **So I decided there is nothing better than to enjoy food and drink and to find satisfaction in work.**
Then I realized that these pleasures are from the hand of God. [25] **For who can eat or enjoy anything apart from him?**

It's because of God that we have abundant blessings.
If you have a job, thank God.
If you have food on the table, thank God.
What are some things in your life that you have
because of your trust and devotion to God?

Notes---

Work Like a Boss... Act Like a Lady...Live Like a Believer

My Prayers:

Answers to Prayer:

MATTHEW 11: 28-29

[28] **Then Jesus said, Come to me, all of you who are weary and carry heavy burdens, and I will give you rest.**
[29] **Take my yoke upon you.**
Let me teach you, because I am humble and gentle at heart, and you will find rest for your souls.

There's a peace that is unexplainable
when you decide to finally let go of
every little piece of worry and doubt.
Trust… it's so difficult, yet so liberating.
What is holding you back from
completely trusting your life to God?

Notes---

My Prayers:

Answers to Prayer:

MARK 6:31
**[31]Then Jesus said, Let's go off by ourselves
to a quiet place and rest awhile.
He said this because there were so
many people coming and going that
Jesus and his apostles didn't even have time to eat.**

When you do what you love, it's easy to get wrapped up in everything that is going on. Don't forget to take a day to give your mind, body, and soul a chance to heal, energize, and prepare for the next week.

You have so much to offer, but only if you have the energy and endurance to do so. Find a quiet place, away from the deadlines and emotions, and reconnect with your Father, who only longs to have a relationship with you. Once you are grounded and refreshed in your spirit, you can once again continue to work on your life's mission.

Notes--

Work Like a Boss... Act Like a Lady...Live Like a Believer

My Prayers:

Answers to Prayer:

CPSIA information can be obtained
at www.ICGtesting.com
Printed in the USA
LVHW080155170619
621430LV00020B/448/P

9 781522 896968